TO:

FROM:

ATTENTION
MANAGEMENT

HOW TO CREATE SUCCESS
AND GAIN PRODUCTIVITY—
EVERY DAY

MAURA NEVEL THOMAS

simple truths
▶ Small books. BIG IMPACT.

IGNITEREADS
spark impact in just one hour

Photo Credits
Internal images © end sheets, page ii, Westend61/Getty Images; page x, Martin
Steinthaler/Getty Images; page xxi, Utamaru Kido/Getty Images; page xxiv, Adam
Kuylenstierna/EyeEm/Getty Images; page 3, PixelCatchers/Getty Images; page 12,
Bernd Vogel/Getty Images; page 36, Tetra Images - Erik Isakson/Getty Images; page
43, gilaxia/Getty Images; page 48, Hero Images/Getty Images; page 56, Hinterhaus
Productions/Getty Images; page 66, Image Source TAC/Getty Images; page 68, Cavan
Images/Getty Images; page 73, Peathegee Inc/Getty Images

Internal images on pages vi, xxvi, 16, 20, 22, 28, 50, 60, 79, and 82 have been
provided by Pexels and Pixabay; these images are licensed under CC0 Creative
Commons and have been released by the author for public use.

Published by Simple Truths, an imprint of Sourcebooks
P.O. Box 4410, Naperville, Illinois 60567-4410
(630) 961-3900
sourcebooks.com

Printed and bound in China.
OGP 10 9 8 7 6 5 4 3 2 1

This book is dedicated to my mentor, friend, and colleague, Dr. Valerie Young, for planting the seed of "focus management" more than twenty years ago.

It's also dedicated to Dr. John ("Uncle Jack") Dovidio, for being a positive influence in my life, a guide and teacher in my professional career, and my go-to source for help understanding the technical aspects in my work.

TABLE OF

CONTENTS

→ DEAR READER,

Thank you for your interest in *Attention Management*! My entire professional career has been about helping busy people improve their productivity, which I define as the ability to make progress on the results that are most significant to you, personally and professionally.

I know that smart, driven people like you have unique gifts to bring to the world, but it's hard to offer those gifts when you are overworked, overtired, and overwhelmed. And my pursuit of productivity has led me to the discovery that time is not our problem, as we all have the same twenty-four hours in a day, and we can't control time.

Our problem now is one of distraction—from our ever-present technology and its ability to deliver communication and information to us in unlimited ways all the time. This, in turn, has created expectations of immediate and constant availability, further fueling our need to stay connected, and therefore, our constant distraction. And since distraction is our problem, "time management" is not the solution. The antidote to distraction is attention. Our ability to manage our attention is our most important defense against a world that is constantly conspiring to steal it.

The competition for your attention has never been more heated. You can't purchase a product or service you've never heard of, so before a company can get your business, they must first get your attention. And this is increasingly difficult with so much "noise."

There is continual innovation around ways to creatively capture your attention, with:

+ in-app and on-page advertising,
+ "advertainment,"
+ the proliferation of immediate communication tools,
+ push notifications,
+ and the rise of "free" services that aren't *really* free but whose cost is actually your attention: the ability to serve you advertising (think Facebook and Google).

All of this means that attention is now our most valuable commodity. This is important to know if you are in business. However, as an individual, it's critical to recognize that your only defense against this assault on your attention is your ability to control it. *This* is what I call attention management and why it's the most important skill for you to master. It's important now, and it will only become more important in the future.

I am on a quest to solve those symptoms of distraction: feeling overworked, overtired, overstressed, and overstimulated. And to provide busy, driven people with tools and strategies to regain control of their lives and work so that they can live lives of *choice* rather than lives full of reaction and distraction. You *can* do more of the things that matter most to you and offer your unique gifts to the world every day. You *can* feel inspired and energized by your active life instead of stressed and overwhelmed. This book is my latest effort in support of that purpose. I am so happy you chose to read it, and I'm excited for you to experience all the benefits of attention management!

INTRODUCTION

THE NEW PATH TO PRODUCTIVITY AND LIVING A LIFE OF CHOICE

The simple act of paying positive attention to people has a great deal to do with productivity.

—TOM PETERS

Where does the time go?

We all seem to find ourselves wondering this more and more these days, and we keep looking for ways to get some of that time back. In your social media feeds right now, there are probably posts about the latest "productivity hack" or an app or gadget that promises to help you squeeze more into your day. An internet search on "improve productivity" returns 211 *million* results.

The problem is that we're thinking about productivity *all wrong*, and that's messing up our lives. We're hung up on the old-fashioned idea of managing time, but to live the lives we really want to live, what we actually need to master is managing our *attention*.

That's a big shift, but now more than ever before, it's an important one to make. In my over two decades of studying, teaching, and writing about productivity, I've come to realize that we're now in a new world. A world that is never "off." A world where there will always be more work, streaming, or socializing we can instantly access to fill our time. That's why we need modern solutions to our modern challenges—and a big update to our thinking.

Through my work, I've seen that the overwhelming amount of time management advice available isn't doing much to improve our lives. We're never going to *make* enough time to do what we should do—or want to do—during the day.

But I've also seen that once my clients recognize the power of attention management, individuals and teams become happier, healthier, and more productive. This is why I wanted to tell a larger audience about attention management, and it's how this book ended up in your hands.

My goal is to explain exactly what attention management is, why it's so vital for your productivity and well-being, and how to master it. I want to support you in transforming your work and life into the vision *you create* for yourself by mastering control over your attention.

First, let's look at why today's world of work makes attention management so essential.

Losing the Battle against Distraction

Let's face it: technology is necessary for all of us but especially for busy professionals. Most of the time, we love it. I bet you're never far from an internet-connected smartphone, tablet, laptop, or e-reader. I bet you often use several of these devices at once! However, here's the downside the business world prefers not to talk about: those devices—and the content we view on them—are intentionally designed to steal your attention.

An app or a website is considered successful when you spend a long time on it and/or come back to it frequently. In fact, your "addiction" is the ultimate goal,[1] and developers are using persuasive technology and drawing on neuroscience and behavioral psychology to deliberately encourage certain behaviors (like scrolling…and scrolling and scrolling!) while discouraging others (like conveying and absorbing thoughtful, nuanced ideas).[2]

Here's the bottom line: The job of the internet is to keep you on the internet. We're stuck in a productivity paradox: we need these tools to do our jobs, but the job of these tools is to keep us using the tools at the expense of doing our jobs...or anything else!

Just think about all the ways we can communicate through technology:

▶ Voice and video calls

▶ Texts

▶ Emails

▶ Social media

▶ Chat and other instant messages

Then combine that with all the ways websites and other technology tools entice you to stay engaged and manipulate your attention:

▶ Links to other articles embedded in news sites

▶ Videos and advertising around the edges of web pages and in apps

▶ Push notifications so you can receive "important information" (which really isn't important)

▶ Videos that auto-start at the end of videos you choose to watch, and other ways they eliminate natural stopping points to keep you engaged

▶ The ability of devices to vibrate, ping, and flash lights (we're wired to notice lights, sound, color, and motion)

▶ "Likes" and other feedback that appeal to our inherent need for social reinforcement

▶ Gamification of behaviors, offering rewards to keep up "streaks" (called the "endowed progress effect")

We invite this constant stream of distraction into our lives through the gadgets we happily embrace. On top of all that, we still have the typical offline distractions, including other people, commercials, and sneaky advertising, and our own restless minds worrying about other things we need to be doing. (This is a big one.)

So is it really a surprise that we are flustered, frazzled, and forgetful?

To stay on top of it all, we've come up with coping mechanisms like checking our phones while driving, during our kids' sporting events, and sometimes even in the middle of the night!

But these behaviors don't help. In fact, they actually *undermine* our ability to live a life of *choice*—rather than a life of reaction and distraction—and to do what matters most to us both personally and professionally.

When you change what you're doing in response to every incoming distraction, you never get the quiet, uninterrupted time you need to get in "flow"—that immersive, highly focused state where you both do your **best** work *and* feel most satisfied by your work.

Furthermore, if part of your attention is always lured away by these distractions, your mind never gets the calm, restful time it needs to recharge. As a result, you get cranky, impatient, and scattered, and your judgment, learning, creativity, and problem-solving abilities suffer.

It's sad and ironic, isn't it? The very things you're doing in the pursuit of productivity sabotage the qualities that help you accomplish what's most important to you.

That's why a shift in our thinking is so urgent. Living the life you want to live—instead of one that just happens to you—depends on it.

Forget What You Know about Time Management

Most of what you've previously learned about how to be more productive—and what many training programs and media articles continue to teach—isn't effective in today's distraction-filled world.

As I mentioned earlier, time management remains the most common approach to productivity. Back in the not-too-distant past, time management techniques really did help with keeping a handle on your workload and getting more done. You could start every morning making a list of things to do that day; assign A, B, and C priorities (or make appointments with yourself on your calendar); and feel confident that you could address the majority of your priorities during your workday. If you got behind, you could always close your office door so you could really focus.

But as the nature of work changed, time management ideas didn't. Today, they are outdated. If you still make a list every morning, it probably becomes obsolete as soon as you check your email. We all grapple with an influx of communication previous generations couldn't have imagined, and everything seems urgent. That makes it harder to prioritize. And these days, having an office door to close is a rare luxury. More likely, you try to work amid the hum of an open office and endless drop-ins by your coworkers.

Even when you set aside time to tackle an important task, you probably still work on it in two-minute increments while you react to your constant emails, text messages, instant messages, and notifications. So at the end of the time you've set aside, the task still isn't done, or it's so full of mistakes that you need extensive revisions.

That's why time management is less useful today than attention management. If you've ever felt frustrated because you never have enough time, can't increase your productivity, or aren't making enough progress on your important goals, this is probably why: how you manage your time is only relevant to the extent that you also devote your *attention*.

What Attention Management Looks Like

When you incorporate the principles of attention management, you'll recognize when your attention is being stolen (or has the potential to be stolen) and make smart choices about your focus and your actions. You'll feel more in control, and you'll be more intentional and less reactive.

This might be hard to imagine, because it's so contrary to today's frantic, "always on" culture that has us impatient, fidgety, and tethered to our devices— but that's why it's so *necessary*.

Start imagining a different way to work and live. Here's how it might look for you:

▶ Although you work in an open office, you're less affected by the noise and interruptions and can stay deeply engaged in your work. You work faster, do better work, and enjoy your work more.

► You take opportunities to rest your mind and inject moments of calm into your day. This makes you feel more creative and inspired, and you generate more insights and solutions.

► You no longer feel controlled by your devices.

► You work less and have more leisure time.

► You give your full attention to your friends, family, hobbies, and recreation. People appreciate how present you are with them. As a result, you feel less burned out and more motivated and inspired when you're back at work.

► You're more engaged in the moments in your life and find them richer and more satisfying.

► You feel more in control and less stressed and impatient.

If you're a leader who can help create a culture of attention management within your team, office, or company, you can expect system-wide results, including:

▶ Higher engagement and improved morale

▶ Greater employee retention

▶ Faster progress toward the key business goals

▶ More creative and innovative work

▶ A calmer pace and less stressed office environment

I'm thrilled about your interest in attention management and excited to help you reap the benefits. I welcome you to a place where exhaustion is optional, where you realize your most important goals for your life and your work, and where you offer your talents and wisdom to the world in a way that motivates, energizes, and inspires you.

ONE

WHAT IS ATTENTION MANAGEMENT— AND WHY IS IT DIFFERENT?

———

Remember then: there is only one time that is important—now! It is the most important time because it is the only time when we have any power.

—LEO TOLSTOY

If you read the introduction, I bet you're beginning to realize you might need a deep shift in your habits and thinking and are intrigued by the potential of attention management. Before you start putting attention management into action, I want to help you thoroughly understand what it is, why it's important, and how it differs from other practices and mental states.

Psychologist and philosopher William James was onto the ideas behind attention management back in the nineteenth century: "*[Attention] is the taking possession by the mind, in clear and vivid form, of one out of what seem several simultaneously possible objects or trains of thought.*"[3]

The key word there is "one." You can't give your attention simultaneously to all of the things that demand it. Attention management allows you to be more proactive than reactive. It means *you* decide where your attention goes instead of letting outside demands decide for you.

The ability to maintain control over your thoughts and actions, rather than inadvertently relinquishing it, is your defense against the damage our fast-paced, technology-rich, always-on environment does to our minds, bodies, and souls—it's essential for living the life you want to lead.

Consider another quote from William James: *"My experience is what I agree to attend to."*

In other words, your attention determines the experiences you have, and when looking back on your life, it's easy to see that the experiences you have determine the life you live. Therefore, you must control your attention to control your life. Since productivity is about directing your activities to the things that are important to *you*, attention management is the logical path to get you there.

Attention management isn't a single behavior. Instead, it's the collective practice of a group of behaviors. There are four general quadrants of attention management, based on how attentive you're being and how much control you are exerting. You have mastered control over your attention when you can routinely recognize which quadrant you're in and make appropriate changes, depending on what you're doing and what you want to accomplish. The four quadrants are:

1. Reactive and distracted

2. Flow

3. Daydreaming

4. Focused and mindful

FOUR QUADRANTS OF
ATTENTION MANAGEMENT
FOR PRODUCTIVITY

REACTIVE + DISTRACTED

+ Superficial, divided attention
+ Multitasking
+ Typical state at work, unaware of how distracted we are

EXAMPLE: *Having several computer windows open at once, fielding "drop-ins"*

FLOW

+ Laser-focused
+ Fully absorbed
+ Disengaged from sense of self
+ Effortless

EXAMPLE: *Doing something you're trained for and good at*

DAYDREAMING

+ Choosing not to focus on anything in particular
+ Little external stimulus
+ Mind-wandering
+ Restorative for your brain

EXAMPLE: *"In-between" moments where you don't take out your phone (e.g., walking, waiting in line)*

FOCUSED + MINDFUL

+ Fully present
+ Deliberately avoiding distraction
+ Making an effort to maintain attention for an extended period of time

EXAMPLE: *A job interview, a thoughtful task or creative activity, watching a movie at a theater*

low

CONTROL

high

low ATTENTION *high*

Distraction vs. Flow

Have you ever been so engrossed in your work or another activity and completely lost track of yourself as time seemed to fly? And at the end of the task, you felt a sense of satisfaction—like you had really accomplished something?

If so, you've experienced the psychological state known as flow. The idea of flow has become one of the most fascinating and influential in business thanks to the work of Mihaly Csikszentmihalyi (pronounced "Me-high Cheek-sent-me-high"), a Hungarian-American psychologist. You may have seen his wildly popular 2004 TED Talk on the topic. He's also the author of *Flow: The Psychology of Optimal Experience*.

Csikszentmihalyi and others describe flow as a state of heightened focus and immersion in an experience—concentration is effortless, performance and achievement are maximized, and a feeling of spontaneous joy results.

This goes against our tendency to perceive

cognitively demanding tasks as harder and unpleasant. Instead, Csikszentmihalyi's work shows that immersion in challenging activities allows us to experience more joy and satisfaction in our work. Flow isn't exclusively related to work, but when we are in a flow state at our jobs, we do our best, most creative work, *and* we feel more deeply satisfied with what we are doing.

You achieve flow when your sense of self falls away, because a specific part of the brain disengages.[4] So control isn't a factor, because when you're in flow, focus is effortless. You are fully attentive and absorbed in the task at hand. You can't enter flow at will—it's not a behavior but a state your brain enters all on its own when the right conditions are present.

The problem is that today's distraction-filled workplaces are the enemy of flow. After all, how immersed can you get in an important task when you get a new email alert every thirty seconds or when your workstation is in the middle of a lively, noisy, open office? If you're like the majority of my clients and people

I speak with, you spend most of your time at work being reactive and distracted. You find it challenging to give your full attention to anything for more than a few minutes at a time, because your attention is being stolen by every new email that comes in, every new ping of your device, every coworker who walks by your desk. You have a dozen computer windows open, you're switching through several throughout the day, and every task in front of you is partly done. Writer Linda Stone coined a term that describes this state well: "continuous partial attention."[5]

When your attention is fractured like this, you may not realize how scattered you are and how much it's undermining your productivity. Too much time here leads to days that feel busy and tiring but are unproductive and unfulfilling. Working like this also chips away at your attention span, so instead of being engrossing and satisfying, any activity that requires focused thought starts to feel more like an impossible mission.

Focus and Mindfulness Require Control

Since flow is a brain state, not a behavior, you can't enter a flow state at will. But what you *can* do is create an ideal environment. Focus is required, and it takes effort to stay focused in part because the constant distractions that fill our lives make us impatient. We're so used to distractions that we get antsy when we don't have them! When we need to focus and think deeply—for example, on a high-impact work project or important conversation—we don't really want to, and we're not very good at it.

All the technology we constantly interact with has made us used to fast, short, and simple. We've started thinking of more cognitively demanding activities as difficult and unpleasant (even when this isn't true).

So in order to focus, we must choose to eliminate distractions. Eliminating distractions and engaging your focus are two components required for flow— think of them like a jump start. If you would like to achieve a flow state more often, engage your focus in an environment intentionally free from distraction more often. Entering flow state more often improves your odds of being both more productive *and* happier.

Do you prefer fast, short, and simple? Test yourself: Do you find yourself reading more articles and fewer books? Do you prefer short "top tips" articles to longer, more nuanced explorations of a topic? Do you frequently find that you don't finish things? Do you find yourself doing more quick, easy tasks and putting off longer, more thoughtful activities? If you answered yes to one or more of these questions, it could be because your patience is being undermined, and your brain functioning is being hijacked!

When we're impatient, it's hard to stay present. Mindfulness is a conscious mental state of recognizing the present moment, being aware of the sensations in your body, and acknowledging your thoughts and feelings. Cultivating mindfulness can mean regularly meditating or simply getting in the habit of centering yourself in the present moment. Practicing mindfulness offers a range of benefits and is a popular way to improve productivity and enhance health.

When you practice mindfulness, it becomes easier to engage your focus. You're better able to recognize those times when you *intend* to be present in a moment or experience but instead allow your attention to be captured by distractions like email, technology, or other people. You're also better able to direct your attention back to where you want it to be and keep it there.

When you are fully controlling your attention, you can be mindful, present, and focused on the people, tasks, and activities that matter most to you.

Benefits of Daydreaming

The last quadrant of attention is what used to happen in the "in-between" moments, such as walking from your office to your car or waiting in line. These are moments when there isn't a lot of stimulus demanding reaction, and you also aren't focusing on anything in particular. Before smartphones, we had many of these in-between moments throughout our day, but now they have been almost entirely eliminated. Our constant distraction has made us so used to constant stimulation that now, in any pause of activity, we have become conditioned to pull out our phones for stimulation and distraction. Quiet moments feel boring and unproductive, because it seems that we aren't "doing" anything.

Yet this is a misconception and a damaging habit. Your brain needs restorative time to reflect, process, and consolidate information. We need those times when our minds can wander, because often these are the times when insights are generated. Those moments when your mind is wandering can be your most creative. If you've ever had a great idea in the shower, you can understand the restorative benefits of this quadrant of attention!

Parts of a Whole

Your ability to recognize when you're in each of these quadrants—reactive and distracted, focused and mindful, daydreaming, and flow—and adjust accordingly based on what's important to you is the practice of attention management. Consider the ideal percentage of your time you'd like to spend in each quadrant. This may depend on the nature of your work and your priorities for your life. The ideas in the rest of this book will help you to adjust your percentages to better serve you. This attention management practice will help you live a life of choice rather than one of reaction and distraction and allow you to maximize your mental capacity, absorb more, and learn better.

Are you ready to unleash your genius?

ATTENTION MANAGEMENT
IS THE ABILITY TO...

UNLEASH YOUR GENIUS

BE PRESENT IN YOUR MOMENTS

CONTROL YOUR DISTRACTIONS

ENGAGE YOUR FLOW

MAXIMIZE YOUR FOCUS

ACHIEVE YOUR SIGNIFICANT RESULTS

ACTION STEPS

+ Continuing your learning on flow and mindfulness will help you get better at attention management. For more on Mihaly Csikszentmihalyi, visit maura thomas.com/flow. For more on mindfulness, visit maurathomas.com/mindfulness.

+ Read more about how time management is failing us and how attention management puts you in control of your life by visiting maurathomas.com/controlyourlife.

+ See on page 19 the abbreviated version of the four quadrants of attention management. In each quadrant, write the amount of time in a given day you think you spend in each quadrant (be honest!). How well do you think this percentage split serves you? Then make a note of what you think is the ideal split for you.

+ Jot down a few examples of any habits you have around focus, mindfulness, daydreaming, and flow. If you don't currently have any, imagine a time you may have achieved flow. It could have been when you were engaged in a hobby, in a creative project, during sports, or another time that you were so engrossed in something the time passed quickly, you were unaware of almost everything else, and you really enjoyed it. Write down the circumstances, such as where you were, who else was around, what time of day it was, how you felt, and what you achieved. Identifying these circumstances will serve as an inspirational reminder and help you to replicate the experience in other parts of your life.

FOUR QUADRANTS OF
ATTENTION MANAGEMENT
FOR PRODUCTIVITY

REACTIVE + DISTRACTED	**FLOW**
CURRENT:	**CURRENT:**
IDEAL:	**IDEAL:**
DAYDREAMING	**FOCUSED + MINDFUL**
CURRENT:	**CURRENT:**
IDEAL:	**IDEAL:**

CONTROL

low

high

low   ATTENTION   high

TWO

ATTENTION MANAGEMENT PROBLEMS UNDERMINE YOUR SUCCESS

What information consumes is rather obvious: it consumes the attention of its recipients. Hence a wealth of information creates a poverty of attention.

—HERBERT SIMON

Now it's time to take a closer look at how attention management—or the lack of it—shapes your work and your life daily. You may be surprised to learn how common work behaviors actually make you

unproductive, stressed, and unsatisfied. "But I have to work this way," you might protest. "This is just how my office is." However, these unhealthy habits and behaviors are just symptoms of distraction, and they are truly optional. This means you can transform your experience at work—and improve your life overall—by sharpening your attention management skills.

Here are some common situations that sabotage productivity and attention management. How many have you experienced or observed?

Distractions Take Over

Do you constantly feel that it's impossible to get anything done because of all the drop-ins and "got a minutes?" you must deal with? My clients tell me one of their biggest distractions is being interrupted by what I call "OPPs"—other people's problems—that they are constantly asked to weigh in on.

You know those times when you're sitting at your desk, just starting to feel immersed in an important task, and then you hear your name? Instantly, your attention shifts from your task to the interrupter as they begin telling you about an issue they want your help with. When they (finally!) leave, research shows it could take several minutes to more than an hour to get back to where you were with your work and begin to make progress again.[6] Even worse, when you expect interruptions, you tend to work faster, and this increases your stress and frustration.[7]

Technology is another major distraction. You're dealing with a massive influx of information that was hard to imagine even fifteen years ago. Myriad information channels—email, texts, social media, and on and on, along with your nagging impulse to check them constantly for something new—compete for your attention when you're trying to focus on important work.

Even our physical environments steal our focus. Our work spaces have become less supportive of productivity. More and more of us work in open office settings that aim to foster collaboration, but they end up hampering focused work. Just think about how many times you've lost your train of thought when activity near your desk distracts you.

Without attention management skills, all the little distractions in your day become a big drain on your productivity and your happiness. You spend your day multitasking, which may make you feel productive, but it actually slows down your work, causes you to make more mistakes, and results in many things done "part way" and almost nothing done to completion (the "reactive and distracted" quadrant from the last chapter). This saps the satisfaction from your work. Psychologists and researchers Theresa Amabile and Steve Kramer coined the phrase *the progress principle* to summarize their findings that, "of all the things that can boost emotions, motivation, and perceptions during a workday, the single most important is making progress in meaningful work. And the more frequently people experience that sense of progress, the more likely they are to be creatively productive in the long run."[8]

Attention management skills are critical to taking back control. They allow you to refocus your day on *your* priorities, so you can make progress on your meaningful work instead of reacting to every incoming demand on your attention.

Unproductive Cultures Take Root

When employees are stressed, disengaged, and unpro-ductive, their problems are typically blamed on poor organization or time management skills. But the actual cause is often an organizational issue that discourages the practice of attention management.

A few examples of how this can play out:

▶ **Employees are tethered to email.** Whether managers intend this or not, there are countless offices where employees think they're being judged on how quickly they answer emails or whether they respond to emails sent after-hours. With this laser focus on responsiveness, the quality of their other, more important work suffers because they can't give it sustained, deep attention.

▶ **Managers evaluate employees based in part on how much time they log at the office.** As a result, the company has a bias against hiring or retaining outstanding employees who need to work remotely full or part time. This happens when managers think productivity requires face time in the office. In reality, employees with good attention management and workflow management skills can work productively anywhere, and those employees who lack those skills will underperform no matter where they work.

▶ **Busyness (rather than actual productivity) is a badge of honor.** An office where everyone is always "putting out fires" is not a productive one. Yet how often do you hear colleagues bragging about how busy they are? How often do you engage in this behavior yourself? Constant, frantic activity doesn't mean that your office is fast-paced and exciting. It just means you work amid chaos. Behaviors that would actually help you prevent some of those fires—like planning and deep thinking—end up feeling like a luxury that you can't afford to indulge.

When an organization's leaders foster employees' ability to manage attention, the team will get more important work done and their morale will improve. Ensuring that the right messages are sent about things like communication procedures, managing for results rather than time on task, and being productive rather than busy will pay huge dividends for an organization's bottom line.

Burnout and Exhaustion Stifle Progress

The most insidious thing about today's workplaces is that they seem to suck the very life out of us. They encourage habits—such as moving fast, constantly checking communication channels, and multitasking—that wear us out and invade our lives outside the office. The pace of our work speeds up our personal lives and throws us into a downward spiral.

So how did we get to this state? It's the inevitable result of distractions, constant communications, and the pace of our work environments. We've lost sight of the importance of attention, along with the ability to manage our own. Our brain function evolves slowly in comparison to the lightning pace of technological advancement. We can try to keep up, and for a while, it may even seem fun, but the futility inevitably catches up with us and takes its toll.

Let's take the common practice of staying plugged into the office 24/7—in other words, never taking your attention away from work for any significant stretch of time. That may *sound* admirable, but it's actually reducing your effectiveness. To be healthy and to do your best work, you must devote attention to the rest of your life. Enjoying friends, family, and the activities you love recharges your energy and enthusiasm for your job and also makes you more creative when you go back to work. Think about it this way: you can't get a fresh perspective on something you never step away from.

Don't forget resting. If you check your phone during the night, then your sleep suffers. When that happens, your judgment gets worse, and you're not as good at performing daily tasks. You don't solve problems or execute plans as well, and you're prone to making errors at work. Beyond a good night's rest, you also need little pauses in your day. If you use all your spare moments to check email, news, or social media, that isn't much of a break at all. Here's why the daydreaming quadrant from chapter one is important, according to cognitive neuroscientist Sandra Bond Chapman:

The frontal lobe brain networks—responsible for reasoning, planning, decision-making, and judgment—work for you in creative ways when the brain is quiet, not while you are effortfully trying to find a solution to a problem. Moments of insight increase as the brain unwinds. Why? When not actively tackling a task, the brain connects random ideas and consolidates these with prior knowledge into exciting new thoughts, ideas, directions, and potential solutions.[9]

Even if your daily habits are solid, you're still at risk for exhaustion, burnout, and dampened creativity and motivation if you never take your attention away from work for longer periods, like weekends and vacations. Unfortunately, the average American worker takes only half of their vacation days.[10] It's also a problem that today's definition of "vacation" seems to entail monitoring email regularly and even checking in with colleagues once a day. Even if you're in touch with the office for just a few minutes per day while on vacation, your attention is likely to stay on work issues for longer than that. This is damaging in several ways:

▶ You're not fully absorbed in the unique and recharging experiences vacations provide, and you may be missing special moments and the opportunity to create lasting memories.

▶ You're depriving yourself of the fresh perspective and creativity boost that being truly away from work can bring.

▶ When you are run down or stressed out, it's harder to manage your attention.

Without attention management, you're more likely to behave in ways that undermine your productivity, mood, health, and mental abilities, and sabotage your capacity to have fulfilling and joyful experiences daily.

ACTION STEPS

+ Learn more about how to manage your attention through workflow management at maurathomas .com/workflowmanagement.

+ Learn more about the benefits of vacation and how you and your company can maximize paid time off by downloading the information packet at maurathomas.com/vacation.

+ Here's an activity to try for at least fourteen days: At the end of each day, make a note of how you feel about the day. Did you end it with a feeling of satisfaction and accomplishment? Did you feel busy and productive or just busy? Do you feel exhausted, energized, or something else? Also include some general notes about how you spent the day, such as meetings, conversations, planned or random tasks, putting out "fires," responding to email and other communication, or big chunks of important work. (If it's hard for you to remember what you did during the day, that's a red flag that you spent it primarily in "reactive and distracted" mode.) Lastly, note how many hours you spent at work or engaged in work activities. (Checking emails from your smartphone counts!)

See if your activities correlate to your feelings about the day and how you feel at the end of the week. This should give you some insight into how you control your attention, how that makes you feel, and where you can make improvements so you can enjoy your work and life more. In the coming chapters, I'll provide specific strategies to improve your attention management skills.

TOP 10 SIGNS
THAT YOU NEED TO MASTER
ATTENTION MANAGEMENT

1. Distractions run your day

2. Regularly handle email or other work after-hours

3. Work while on vacation

4. Multitask as a coping strategy

5. Available for work 24/7/365

6. Think "I can sleep when I'm dead"

7. Busyness is a badge of honor

8. Loved ones are frequently annoyed by your relationship with your smartphone

9. Work in an open office environment

10. Frequently exhausted and/or overwhelmed

THREE

STARTING YOUR JOURNEY WITH ATTENTION MANAGEMENT

The little things? The little
moments? They aren't little.

—JON KABAT-ZINN

Now let's get into the specifics about how to practice attention management. When I teach attention management inside companies, I start by teaching people to control their technology and to control their environment.

Control Your Technology

Do you ever feel like you serve your devices instead of the other way around? We seem to have forgotten we purchase our technology for *our* convenience, not so anyone in the world has the convenience of interrupting us at any time!

To reverse this trend, we must regain control over our technology. Following are some simple ways to do this.

First, remember that every device has an off button! When was the last time you used one? Constant alerts and notifications have accustomed you to distraction, and this is chipping away at your attention span. Turning your phone (or tablet) off when you're doing other things will eventually reduce your dependence on it. At first, you'll be tempted to reach for your device constantly. But then you'll remember it's off and leave it be. Eventually, you won't even think about it for long stretches. You'll stop allowing your phone to distract you every few minutes. And you'll reverse the erosion of your attention span and strengthen your ability to focus for longer periods. You'll find it easier to spend time in the focused and mindful quadrant.

If you're concerned about an emergency or about the ability of family members to reach you when they need something important, consider whether they have other means than your cell phone. Do you have a phone in your office or a receptionist or paging system at your company? Also, you can certainly turn your phone on and check it periodically at times you determine in advance. The important difference is that you'll be more likely to do that *in between* other tasks rather than *during* other tasks. That will make all the difference in your application of your brain power, the quality of your output, and the time it takes you to get things done.

If you can't quite bring yourself to turn your phone off, you can try some of these tips:

► Learn how to use your phone's Do Not Disturb mode. This allows you to receive calls and texts only from certain numbers, or it will allow numbers that have made multiple calls in a short period of time to ring through.

▶ You may already be using the vibrate feature when you don't want others to hear your phone ring, but try setting it to silent instead (silent without vibrate *is* possible). Vibration means *you* still know you have a call or message (even if others don't), and that's hijacking your attention.

▶ Use airplane mode more often, especially when you go to bed. This allows you to still access the features of your phone that you may need—such as music, white noise, or the alarm clock—without being interrupted by incoming calls and messages.

▶ Change the settings on your email client and apps to download email only when you click. (Sometimes called "Fetch, Manual.")

▶ On your computer, close your email client when you can, or work in offline mode at all times except periods you've specifically allocated to working through emails.

▶ Shut off all but the most critical notifications (and no, breaking news and your social media likes aren't critical).

Lastly, while your phone is off, keep it out of sight and far away. **A study of eight hundred smartphone users showed that just the presence of our devices is distracting**. In tests of cognitive ability, people whose phones were in another room significantly outperformed people whose phones were in their pockets and slightly outperformed those whose phones were in nearby bags.[11]

These techniques will help you handle your digital distractions, but technology isn't the only attention thief. The next step is equally as important.

Control Your Environment— Managing Others

Whether you work in an open office, at home, or from different locations on the road, your physical environment has a big effect on how well you manage your attention.

We often behave as if we are at the mercy of our noisy, distracting environments (such as an open-concept workspace). But we have more control than we realize. These strategies can help you prevent your attention from being stolen.

Make a "do not disturb" sign to hang on your office door, the back of your chair, or a cubicle wall when you are trying to focus. This prevents the inevitable "Do you have a minute?" drop-ins. (Adding a touch of humor to your sign helps get colleagues on board.)

Besides shutting out the noise around you, headphones also send a visual signal to others that you'd prefer not to be interrupted. However, what you play in those headphones matters. If you do your

best work in quiet, use noise-canceling headphones. If you prefer some background noise, studies show that music with lyrics is very distracting if you're reading, studying, or writing.[12] Better choices for improved performance are classical or other music without lyrics, white noise, or "binaural beats," a type of music shown to induce certain states of mind.

If you leave your sign up or your headphones on all day, every day, they will lose their effectiveness. If you work with others, you'll need to be available at least some of the time. Also, if you convey the message that you prefer not to be disturbed, then people interrupt you anyway, and you give them what they need, that's teaching them that you aren't serious about the message. You have to honor the boundaries you create and use them judiciously. When you do, your coworkers will fall in line.

Another option is to move to a quieter part of your office when you need to do focused work. If there's no such place in your office, that's a problem. Start a conversation with your managers and colleagues—or if you work from home, your family or roommates—about how you can create spaces that support different kinds of work.

If you work at home, it's distracting to work in a place that is typically devoted to other things. You're unlikely to do your best work at the dining room table or on the living room couch, and it will blur the lines between work time and personal time. Instead, have a dedicated space that is used only (or at least mostly) for work.

Control Your Environment— Managing Clutter

A cluttered workspace is a subtle source of stress, and it means that other work and other issues will be calling to you when you're trying to focus. If there is a mess on your desk, at least put it in a pile, in a box, or in a folder marked "to process." This will reduce the chances that the clutter will steal your attention.

If you're thinking, "But, Maura, I know where everything is! I can't move it!" then it's time for a new strategy for handling your clutter. You may, in fact, know where everything is, but you're relying on your brain to remember, and that's stressful!

The suggestions in this chapter may feel foreign to you, and they may temporarily confuse others if they are used to you behaving differently. But let's face it—they aren't hard, and they'll improve your work and personal life in a big way. While others might give you a hard time initially, it's only because you have set the expectation that you are always available. Once they get used to your new boundaries, they will behave accordingly.

In fact, the mere act of becoming more aware of your distractions will help you to get better at attention management. Eckhart Tolle, the spiritual teacher made famous by Oprah, has said, "Awareness is the greatest agent for change." When you start noticing that you're being interrupted and think to yourself, *I should have closed my door* or *I should have put my phone on Do Not Disturb*, it won't be long before attention-managing behaviors follow.

Once you've begun to regain control over the distractions that come via your technology and your environment, it will be time to tackle the bad habits you've likely formed as a coping mechanism to deal with all these distractions. In the next chapter, I'll give you strategies and techniques for controlling your habits and your thoughts.

ACTION STEPS

+ Ensure that your workspace is set up to minimize clutter and distraction by downloading the resource at maurathomas.com/clutter.

+ Make a list of the suggestions in this chapter you can implement easily. When exactly will you try each one? Do you have an upcoming occasion—like an evening out with friends or a walk with a spouse or child—where you can leave your phone at home? Can you make a "do not disturb" sign for your desk right now? (Check the internet if you need ideas for creative signs.) What challenges might arise when you implement these changes? How will you prevent or overcome those challenges? Making a plan will improve the odds that you will take action and stick with the behaviors when problems arise. Taking one action also increases the odds that you'll take another action...and another.

FOUR

HOW TO MASTER ATTENTION MANAGEMENT

We are what we repeatedly do. Excellence,

therefore, is not an act, but a habit.

—WILL DURANT, PARAPHRASING ARISTOTLE

Ready to take your attention management skills to the next level? If you've made good progress with exerting more control over your technology and your environment, then you've taken the first steps toward retraining your mind. The behaviors we'll talk about in this

chapter build on those steps, and they'll have an even deeper impact on your life.

Don't worry, you don't have to implement them all at once or become master of them all. Just getting started will give you an important edge in your life and career. Remember that the ultimate goal of attention management is to unleash the full benefit of your wisdom and brainpower, allowing you to achieve more of your significant results and live a life of *choice* rather than a life of reaction and distraction.

Control Your Habits

Sometimes we really are our own worst enemy! If you've tried any of the strategies described in the last chapter, you may have experienced that cutting out distractions can initially make you feel antsy, anxious, or downright uncomfortable. That's because you've been conditioned into a state of constant distraction. But there are ways to rebuild your attention span and regain control over your focus.

Even if you believe that you thrive on the chaos, you'll find your performance improves when you balance the chaotic times with moments of calm and periods of deep work. You'll also become more satisfied and enjoy more meaningful interactions with other people. Here are some ways to start shifting your behavior and find a more productive balance.

▶ Set a timer for short stretches of time, even just ten minutes. During this time, eliminate all distractions by controlling your environment and your technology. Pick an activity, close out everything else, start the timer, and single-task. Once the time is up, you can take a break or continue working if you're on a roll. Following the break, reset the timer and start the process over. At first, even ten minutes may seem like an eternity, but over time, it will become much more comfortable, and you can increase the stretch of time to fifteen, twenty, thirty minutes and more. Following this practice will help you build up to longer and longer periods of uninterrupted work.

▶ Give yourself some quick pockets of quiet time. See if you can sit relatively still, without speaking, without any devices, and without napping— just letting your mind wander or absorbing the environment around you. This gives your brain the downtime it needs to process information, reflect, and generate insights.[13] At first, you might be unable to do this for even one minute! But it gets easier with practice. Try enjoying your quiet moments outside.

► Get started with mindfulness. You can be mindful (fully present) without meditating, but an easy way to get started with mindfulness is through short, guided meditations. Many apps can help you with this (try the Buddhify, Simple Habit, or Headspace apps). Even just two- to five-minute guided medita-tions can help. The more you meditate, the more you become aware of your thoughts and emotions as they arise, which in turn helps you regulate them and your reactions to them. The ability to recognize an emotion as it happens is the key to your EQ, or emotional intelligence, and your EQ can be more important to your success than your intelligence.[14]

► Spend time every week completely free from technology. When you head outside for a walk or a hike, see a movie, play sports, or have dinner with friends or family, leave your phone at home. You may feel panicky at first. But after you get over the initial shock, you might find it liberating!

► Do some physical activity every day, especially before times when you really need to focus. Movement sends oxygen to your brain, sharpening your focus. If you're at work, take a few minutes to walk up and down the stairs a couple of times before sitting down, setting your timer, and tackling that single task.

► Take regular breaks. Work on one longer task or a series of consecutive tasks (one at a time!) for twenty-five to ninety minutes, and then take a break for five to seventeen minutes. Expert opinion varies on the optimal stretch of time one should work before taking a break,[15] as well as the optimal length for a break. But the truth is, everyone is different, every day is different, and every set of tasks is different. Some people have more energy than others; at some times of the day, you're more energetic than others; and some tasks are more engaging than others. Honor how you're feeling and recognize that a work break can be just as energizing as caffeine or sugar, provided you actually do something different. For example, if you've spent the last sixty minutes reading reports, using your break to read the news or your Facebook feed isn't restorative. Instead, move your body, do a short, guided meditation, or even close your eyes and rest or doze for ten minutes if you can find a private place to do that.

Since a key to entering "flow state," as discussed in chapter one, is the absence of distraction, these attention management behaviors will help you to achieve flow more often—elevating your performance and making your work more satisfying and enjoyable.

Control Your Thoughts

When you become better at recognizing what's going on in your mind, you can start taking steps to actively shape your thoughts. Here are a few techniques to try.

Workflow Management

Picture this scenario: You need to get an important task done. Because you've been building your attention management skills, you know to close your email, turn off your phone, and find a quiet place to work. Perfect! You're ready to get down to business.

But you manage to work only a couple of minutes before thoughts like these start to interfere with your focus:

- *I haven't prepared for the meeting on Thursday.*
- *The fridge was really bare this morning. When can I get to the grocery store?*
- *Team member reviews are due soon, and I haven't started on them.*
- *Don't forget to sign up for that training! The deadline is coming up.*
- *I'm not making any progress on starting my own business.*

The distractions from your own mind can be even more powerful than those from your technology or surroundings, and one of the ways your mind distracts you from the moment at hand is by reminding you of all the other things you need to do, whether over the short term or the long term. Your anxiety about staying on top of everything keeps your mind wandering to incomplete tasks, commitments, responsibilities, uncaptured ideas, and things you aren't doing in that moment. The result is that you can't quiet your mind when you need to rest, and you have a hard time focusing on work or on the people you're with.

The solution comes down to these three truths:

1. You can only manage what you can see.

2. You can only see what's outside your head.

3. You need things in one centralized, external location that you trust and that you can refer to at any time.

Life is just too complex to rely on your memory to track all of your work and personal obligations. When was the last time your mind pulled up the exact information you needed at the exact time you needed it, on command? So the first thing you have to do is get all this information out of your head. You may already do this if you routinely jot notes, reminders, and tasks in notebooks, on sticky notes, or on the random pieces of paper you find on your desk.

However, if your notes, reminders, and tasks are scattered across different places—for example, your email inbox, sticky notes at your work station, and a separate to-do list at home—that still leaves your mind anxious that you might be missing something. To relieve this anxiety, you need to get everything into one place.

You need a systematic, centralized way to handle everything on your plate. This is called a workflow management system.

Learning a workflow management system will relieve stress, quiet your mind, and give you clarity. When you feel assured that all of your responsibilities are captured in one reliable place, you free up a lot of mental space.

Get into Flow

As I mentioned in chapter one, flow is a psychological state where performance is optimized and focus is effortless. It's total absorption in the task at hand, where time passes quickly and a feeling of spontaneous joy can result. We can't will ourselves into flow (our brain isn't obedient that way), but what we *can* do is set up the conditions for flow, thereby increasing the odds it will happen.

As discussed in chapter one, most people don't get into flow very often, in part because they fail to shut out distractions very often—if ever. There are also other ingredients necessary for flow. The task at hand has to be one that you care about. It shouldn't be too easy for you, because if it is, you'll get bored instead of getting into flow. It also shouldn't be beyond your abilities, because then you'll get frustrated instead of getting into flow.

Practicing attention management will help you spend more time in the quadrant of flow. When you do, you'll get more important work done, and you'll get more satisfaction and enjoyment from your work.

Seek Depth

An unfortunate by-product of our harried lives is the loss of depth and nuance. Our growing impatience means we read the summary instead of the book and the headline instead of the story. We think we know a thing or two about a breathtaking number of things, but we don't have more than a passing familiarity with any of them.

When you never go below the surface of all the

information available to you, you miss out on a lot, including the chance to build the kind of rich expertise that makes you stand out from others and gives you an edge in your career. Taking a deep dive into something that intrigues you also expands your thinking, turbo-charges your creativity, and makes you more interesting. As an added bonus, deep learning is another chance to enter a satisfying flow state.

To start reaping those benefits, give yourself some undistracted time to try out these ideas:

▶ Read more books and fewer articles.

▶ If and when you read articles, choose more in-depth pieces that dissect a topic or issue and fewer "listicles" ("Top 10 Ways to XXX," etc.).

▶ Discuss topics that interest you with knowledgeable people. Consider joining groups related to your interests.

▶ Become a better listener. This requires presence, and it will help you to create rapport with others and improve your communications. Author Scott Eblin describes three levels of listening:

  ▸ Transient—focusing more on yourself than on the other person; feeling distracted and impatient.
  ▸ Transactional—focusing on the next step or the solution to a problem.
  ▸ Transformational—establishing connections with and between people and ideas.[16]

Remember, managing your attention by controlling your technology, your environment, your habits, and your thoughts will get easier the more you practice these behaviors. You'll begin to see benefits such as more meaningful interactions with people, more satisfying work, more progress on more of your goals, and ultimately, more success in all parts of your life.

ACTION STEPS

+ Consider a workflow management process for controlling your internal distractions. Download the resources to get started at maurathomas.com/workflowmanagement.

+ Give each day of the week a theme from this chapter. For example:

  ▶ **MONDAY:** single-task using a timer for increasing periods of time during which you can comfortably focus on only one thing.

  ▶ **TUESDAY**: take two breaks during which you sit still, outside if possible, by yourself and without your devices.

  ▶ **WEDNESDAY**: do two short, guided meditations to help you build up to a longer, more frequent practice.

▶ **THURSDAY**: read at least one chapter from a nonfiction book or a long-form article on something that interests you or that you want to become an expert in.

▶ **FRIDAY**: engage in a mentally challenging activity, such as playing chess, taking a class, or learning a new language.

▶ **SATURDAY**: get out in nature for an hour or more and leave your phone behind.

▶ **SUNDAY**: do something with another person you enjoy spending time with. Keep your phones out of sight, practice transformational listening, and offer the other person the gift of your full presence and attention.

FIVE

SET YOURSELF UP FOR SUCCESS WITH ATTENTION MANAGEMENT

———

Your net worth to the world is usually determined by what remains after your bad habits are subtracted from your good ones.

—BENJAMIN FRANKLIN

If you've been trying out some of the Action Steps from previous chapters, I hope you're already seeing how attention management helps you be more productive, less stressed, and more satisfied with your work and life. But I also hope that you'll be patient

and supportive with yourself as you change what are probably some long-entrenched habits. It's hard work! So celebrate the small wins, don't get discouraged, and keep going!

Habits Are Powerful

Think about how many of your daily behaviors are habits. Let's take email as an example. Maybe you automatically log into your email client when you get to work or reflexively check your email every time you get a notification. You've engaged in these behaviors for so long that you practice them without thinking. You're on autopilot.

Even if you understand how attention management behaviors—like turning off notifications or working in offline mode—could benefit you, that doesn't mean you will instantly change. This chapter discusses other ways you can support your success.

Work Drains Willpower

Engaging in your old habits is effortless. But practicing new behaviors takes more energy and intention. Instead of coasting on autopilot, you're paying closer attention to what you're doing, and you're deciding, again and again, to make different choices. All those decisions take willpower. And none of us has an infinite supply.[17]

Let's go back to the example of email use. You might start the week practicing all of your healthy new behaviors. You set aside email-free time for focused work, and you keep your phone out of sight at home so you're not constantly tempted to check it. But after a busy and stressful week, you slip back into your old habits. You find yourself checking email and reaching for your phone without thinking.

So why does this happen? The nature of work today makes it hard to refill our willpower reserves. Amid all the demands on your time, sleep and rest are often the first things to go. And when you never get a chance to recharge, it's harder to perform higher-order mental tasks—like making the choices that support attention management.

If the norm at your office is having doughnuts at meetings, skipping lunch because you're busy, scarfing pizza at every late-night work session, and downing coffee around the clock, your willpower is under attack on another front as well. When you don't eat or hydrate well, you're not giving your brain the fuel it needs to muster enough willpower.

Give Your Brain What It Needs

To build the willpower you need to better manage your attention, practice self-nurturing behaviors like these:

▶ **Prioritize rest of all kinds.** Quit sleeping with your phone by the bed. If your energy flags during the day, grab a nap if you can. Beyond healthy sleep, pause regularly during the day to quiet your mind. Even a brief moment helps. And, as mentioned in chapter two, don't forget about the power of longer breaks. A vacation replenishes your reserves of energy, thoughtfulness, and willpower.

▶ **Fuel up right.** Typical office eating habits can send you on an energy roller coaster of blood sugar highs and crashes. To reduce the temptation of treats like bagels at the morning meeting, keep a stockpile of healthy snacks in your desk or the office fridge that are easy to grab even when you're short on time. Some ideas include baby carrots, hummus, nuts, fruit, cheese cubes or spreads, all-natural granola bars, seltzers, and unsweetened teas. Along with improving your physical health, you'll also empower yourself for the more thoughtful decision-making that is required to stick with your new habits.

▶ **Get outside.** Time outdoors is a powerful mental reset. It's even better if you can move around some while you're outside. Exercise reduces stress, which is widely thought to deplete willpower, especially if you've been sitting all day.

When you practice behaviors like these, you'll be better able to resist the behaviors that don't serve you, like multitasking and constantly checking your devices. You'll more easily correct course and choose a more productive path, like turning off notifications to focus on your most important work.

I want to add a special note for leaders here. Would you rather have an office full of thoughtful, deliberate team members—or one where staffers spend all day reacting to the latest demands on their time and lose sight of the big picture? The answer is obvious, of course. But it's surprising how rarely leaders use their influence to create an environment that supports attention management. You can be an exception. Set up a nap room and encourage employees to use it. Don't email them late at night or while they're on vacation. Stock the break room with healthy snacks. You'll reap the return on this investment many times over in the quality of their work.

Belief in Bad Habits

In *The Power of Habit*, Charles Duhigg writes that belief is an important ingredient in turning a habit into a permanent behavior. Lack of belief in an effective habit or misplaced belief in a less effective habit can lead us astray.

For example, most people have experienced for themselves how satisfying and productive flow state can be, and studies confirm that single-tasking is most effective. However, sometimes damaging behaviors can seem more effective. For example:

▶ Task-switching, or doing many things at once, *seems* like it should lead to getting more done.

▶ Leaving your email open all the time *seems* like the only way to prevent it from overwhelming you.

▶ Allowing constant alerts and notifications *seems* like the only way to avoid missing something important.

The persistent belief that distracted work at a frantic pace is beneficial—or at least necessary—is difficult to overcome. One reason for this is that we undervalue the achievement and overvalue the importance of the interruption. Chaos makes our days feel dynamic and busy, and it's easy to mistake being busy for being productive. But we can only be productive— achieve our significant results—when we can be *pro*active. And we can only be *pro*active when we're not being *re*active.

Take the example of my client "Joe." Joe shared a story about a time when he closed his email so that he could finish an important project. As a result, he didn't respond immediately to an email from his boss about a client issue. When I asked what happened, Joe said that his boss got the information from a coworker. I asked if he got in trouble with his boss (he didn't), if he finished his important project (he did), if the project was more important to the big picture than answering that email immediately (it was), and if he felt a sense of accomplishment when he completed the project (he did). But later, he felt that he had been "beaten out" by his coworker, as if there were some ongoing competition for who was the most responsive. Even Joe's boss confirming he made the right decision didn't prevent the "cost" from overshadowing the success.

It's true that every decision has consequences. But I'm convinced (and my clients' experiences prove) that the benefits of attention management far outweigh the costs, and it might help to think of it the other way: Do the benefits of being the "most responsive" and the temporary excitement you may feel during chaotic, distracted days outweigh the benefits of attention management, such as improved performance, more progress on more goals, and more meaningful communications? In the big picture, do you think you'll advance your career and get evaluated more favorably for answering all of your emails quickly or for your most important work getting done faster, better, and more often?

Overthinking and Stress

As you gain experience with attention management, your new, productive habits will replace your old, damaging ones. You'll be on autopilot again, but this time with healthy behaviors.

Sometimes, however, the habits you've cultivated get disrupted when you're especially busy. Your brain thinks you're in a novel situation that requires a lot of intentional thought and deliberate decisions—which is slower and less effective than relying on your established good habits.

This is what happens when we "choke," Malcolm Gladwell writes in his book *Outliers*. He uses the example of Jana Novotná and her 1993 match against Steffi Graf in the final round at Wimbledon. Near what should have been the end of the tournament, the pressure became too much, and Novotná began to overthink. Instead of relying on the muscle memory and mental habits she had developed in countless hours of practice, she began to second-guess everything, and

at that level of competition, second-guessing every move is disastrous.

When you're under pressure yourself, you may second-guess your attention management habits. *They've worked for me before*, you might think. *But now they'll take too long, and this situation demands a unique response.* You might turn every action into a decision. But in fact, these are the times when it is most useful to rely on these new behaviors that you decided in advance, when your thinking was clear, would serve you.

Start Now

Improving your attention management works much the same way as improving your physical health. For example, you might start off by implementing one healthier habit, like exercise. One change leads to more small shifts, like reading food labels and drinking more water. Eventually, all your small changes combine to create big results. You'll find the same is true for attention management. The more often you tackle and complete larger, more important tasks, the more satisfied you'll feel. As a result, you'll tolerate fewer distractions and do more to control interruptions, because you will have seen the results created by regularly practicing attention management.

Don't focus on the times you don't control your attention. Notice and celebrate the times you do.

ACTION STEPS

+ Talk to the people in your personal and professional life about your new practice of attention management. It will help them to understand your new behaviors and respect your boundaries. Even better, recruit others to join you in the effort. Discuss your successes and hold each other accountable.

+ Each day that you take at least one step from this book, mark your calendar. See if you can create a streak and keep it going. Once the streak gets long, start aiming for two steps and two marks on your calendar per day. Reward yourself for your plentiful marks and your long streaks. This will create a positive cycle that will transform your daily experiences and, ultimately, your life.

CONCLUSION

ATTENTION MANAGEMENT IS THE KEY TO A LIFE OF CHOICE

———————

What matters more than the moments in your life is the life in your moments.

—UNKNOWN

As of this writing, I've been working in the productivity industry for twenty-five years. And the result of that work is my conviction that attention management is the single most important skill for true productivity—the ability to achieve your most significant results, to be the kind of person you want to be, and to live a life of choice rather than a life of reaction and distraction.

I want to leave you with these closing thoughts on attention management:

▶ Attention management is the antidote for the increasingly dysfunctional and unsustainable way we work and live. In a world that's getting more frenetic and reactive, you can take a stand for thoughtfulness, for balance, and for meaningful work by practicing attention management.

▶ Being busy and being productive are very different things.

▶ Productivity doesn't happen by chance. Today's fast-paced world requires us to be more deliberate if we want to accomplish our most important goals. If you allow all the incoming demands on your time to set your agenda, your most meaningful work will languish.

▶ It's no longer an option to work the same way we always have or to teach productivity the same way. Old methodologies like time management and old metrics (like face time in the office) are no longer relevant. Individuals who don't change will burn out. Companies that don't change will fall behind.

▶ The conventional wisdom claiming professional success is impossible without constant, relentless work isn't just unwise—it's incorrect and dangerous. Everything research tells us about doing our best work goes against the "I'll sleep when I'm dead" ethos of all too many workplaces. The truth is that exhaustion is optional!

▶ Both companies and individuals must embrace the idea that the most important resources supporting productivity aren't time and money—they're body and mind. Self-care (or, from the perspective of the company, employee care) isn't a "nice to have." It's *essential*. Any effort to be more productive that doesn't acknowledge the necessity of physical and emotional well-being is destined to fail.

▶ You have more control than you think—over your technology, your environment, and even your own habits and thoughts. Exerting that control is necessary. Attention management is the path to reclaiming it.

▶ Attention management transcends conventional notions of productivity and speaks to our fundamental desire to live a life of our choosing, a life that matters to us. George Lucas reportedly put it this way: "Always remember, your focus determines your reality." Can there be any more important skill to master?

A Life of Choice

Every week, I ask the busy, successful, driven people in my audiences to list the words that they want people to use to describe them. The answers are always shockingly similar and include:

- *Caring*
- *Present*
- *Thoughtful*
- *Loving*
- *Reliable*
- *Fun*
- *Dedicated*
- *Generous*

When I ask what word they most want to represent their life, the answers include:

- *Healthy*
- *Successful*
- *Full*
- *Productive*
- *Satisfying*
- *Grateful*
- *Helpful*
- *Significant*
- *Impactful*
- *Meaningful*

Exemplifying these qualities requires intention—not just at work but when we're being parents, partners, friends, neighbors, volunteers, family members, and all the other roles that we play in our lives.

Intention requires attention management. If your attention determines the experiences you have in your life and the experiences you have make up the life you live, then your attention determines your life.

What if you consistently allow your attention to be stolen by the millions of things that are constantly demanding it? Then you end up with too many days where you felt busy but didn't accomplish much. Those days add up into weeks, months, and years. And eventually, you'll find yourself wondering why you never accomplished your important goals or why you feel disconnected from the important people in your life.

Researchers found that the average knowledge worker switched what they were attending to every three minutes and five seconds.[18]

Three minutes isn't enough time to be fully present

when someone is sharing something important with you. If you glance at your phone, they know you aren't paying attention to them. How might your obvious lack of presence affect your relationships, the quality of your communication, and what the people in your life think of you?

A few minutes isn't enough time to reflect on your accomplishments or be grateful for them. Studies show that gratitude and happiness are highly correlated, but gratitude requires reflection, and reflection requires sustained attention.

A few minutes isn't even enough time to fully appreciate the beauty that's all around you—a storm rolling in, a sunrise or sunset, the twinkle in someone's eye, or the look of wonder on the face of a child.

Every single moment of your life *could* be a moment that you will remember for the rest of your life. Every single moment *could* be the moment that will change your life forever. We usually can't see those moments coming.

In expressing his appreciation for receiving the Nobel Peace Prize, Martin Luther King Jr. said, "Occasionally in life there are those moments of unutterable fulfillment which cannot be completely explained by those symbols called words. Their meanings can only be articulated by the inaudible language of the heart."

If you can't control your attention, you won't be able to speak that inaudible language of the heart. Don't allow distraction to rob you of the moments that make your life worth living. Instead, control your attention to control your life.

ENDNOTES

1   The term "diaper product" is shorthand in the tech industry for a tool so addicting that you don't even want to get up to pee!

2   Haley Sweetland Edwards, "Boundless Mind Wants to Fix America's Smartphone Addiction," *Time*, April 12, 2018, https://time.com/5237434/youre-addicted-to-your-smartphone-this-company-thinks-it-can-change-that/.

3   William James, *The Principles of Psychology* (New York: Henry Holt and Company, 1890), 1:403-404.

4   Daniel Goleman, "Train Your Brain for Flow," LinkedIn, last modified January 30, 2016, https://www.linkedin.com/pulse/train-your-brain-flow-daniel-goleman.

5   Linda Stone, "Beyond Simple Multi-Tasking: Continuous Partial Attention," LindaStone.net, November 30, 2009, https://lindastone.net/2009/11/30/beyond-simple-multi-tasking-continuous-partial-attention/.

6   Kristin Wong, "How Long It Takes to Get Back on Track After a Distraction," *Lifehacker*, July 29, 2015, https://lifehacker.com/how-long-it-takes-to-get-back-on-track-after-a-distract-1720708353.

7   Daniela Gudith, Ulrich Klocke, and Gloria Mark, "The Cost of Interrupted Work: More Speed and Stress," paper presented at ACM CHI 2008, April 2008, https://www.ics.uci.edu/~gmark/chi08-mark.pdf.

8   Teresa Amabile and Steven J. Kramer, "The Power of Small Wins," *Harvard Business Review*, May 1, 2011, https://hbr.org/2011/05/the-power-of-small-wins.

9   Sandra Bond Chapman, "Why Your Mind Needs a Break," *Psychology Today*, June 16, 2014, https://www.psychologytoday.com/us/blog/make-your-brain-smarter/201406/why-your-mind-needs-break.

10   Quentin Fottrell, "The Sad Reason Half of Americans Don't Take All Their Paid Vacation," MarketWatch, May 28, 2017, https://www.marketwatch.com/story/55-of-american-workers-dont-take-all-their-paid-vacation-2016-06-15.

11   "The Mere Presence of Your Smartphone Reduces Brain Power, Study Shows," UT News, June 26, 2017, https://news.utexas.edu/2017/06/26/the-mere-presence-of-your-smartphone-reduces-brain-power.

12   Nick Perham and Harriet Currie, "Does Listening to Preferred Music Improve Reading Comprehension Performance?" *Applied Cognitive Psychology* 28 (January 2014): 279–284, https://doi.org/10.1002/acp.2994.

13   Ferris Jabr, "Why Your Brain Needs More Downtime," *Scientific American*, October 15, 2013, https://www.scientificamerican.com/article/mental-downtime/.

14   Michael Akers and Grover Porter, "What Is Emotional Intelligence (EQ)?" PsychCentral, April 4, 2018, https://psychcentral.com/lib/what-is-emotional-intelligence-eq/.

15   Stephanie Vozza, "This Is How Many Minutes of Breaks You Need Each Day," *Fast Company*, October 31, 2017, https://www.fastcompany.com/40487419/this-is-how-many-minutes-of-breaks-you-need-each-day.

16   Kermit Pattison, "Worker, Interrupted: The Cost of Task Switching," *Fast Company*, July 28, 2008, https://www.fastcompany.com/944128/worker-interrupted-cost-task-switching.

17   New research has called the idea of "willpower reserves" into question, however my point here is more related to "decision fatigue," which is still a valid theory in psychology research.

18   Brigid Schulte, "Overworked and Overwhelmed? Try the Mindfulness Alternative," *Washington Post*, June 22, 2015, https://www.washingtonpost.com/news/inspired-life/wp/2015/06/22/overworked-and-overwhelmed-try-the-mindfulness-alternative.

INDEX

ACKNOWLEDGMENTS

Thank you for reading my book! I've helped business leaders and the knowledge workers they employ improve their productivity for my entire career. And in that time, I've discovered that almost all of them feel overwhelmed, overworked, and overtired. Since we now live in a world of work without walls, where work follows us via our technology, those feelings permeate our personal lives as well.

I am on a quest to change things—to provide busy, driven people with tools and strategies to regain control of their lives and work so that they can live lives of choice rather than reaction. You *can* do more of the things that matter and offer your unique gifts to the world every day. You *can* feel inspired and energized instead of stressed and overwhelmed. This book is my latest effort to support that purpose. I'm grateful to you for reading it and excited for you to realize the benefits!

You can find more information on attention management, including support materials, at my website, MauraThomas.com—as well as information on my previous works to help you tackle individual and organizational productivity and live a happier, more productive, and more intentional life!

A final note of thanks...

Thank you to my editors! Sarah Beckham is a writer, editor, and content marketer based in Austin, Texas. Previously a newspaper features editor, she now uses her twenty years of journalism experience to help business clients tell their stories and spread their ideas. Sarah has a finely honed ability to make my writing clear and concise while still using most of my words and staying true to my original meaning.

Shawn Thomas is a speaker, researcher, and fine art photographer who also happens to be my husband. He uses photography as an external representation of self-reflection and personal growth and as a tool to help others discover their own paths to self-mastery. Shawn had a successful career in the fields of statistics, higher education, and social sciences until joining forces with me to bring his skills and experience to our business, Regain Your Time. He has been published in multiple academic journals and business publications, including the *Harvard Business Review*. Shawn is able to add a perspective from a different way of thinking and help make my points relatable to a wider range of people. This book is vastly improved because of Sarah's and Shawn's input, and I am immeasurably grateful to both of them.

I'd also like to thank the great team at Sourcebooks, especially my editor, Meg Gibbons.

ABOUT THE AUTHOR

Maura Nevel Thomas is an award-winning international speaker, trainer, and author on individual and corporate productivity and work-life balance, and she is the most widely cited authority on attention management.

She helps driven, motivated knowledge workers control their attention and regain control over the details of their life and work. Maura has trained tens of thousands of individuals at thousands of organizations on her proprietary Empowered Productivity™ System, a process for achieving significant results and living a life of choice.

Maura's clients include the likes of Dell, Old Navy, the U.S. Army, L'Oréal, the American Heart Association, and Kaiser Permanente. She is a TEDx speaker, successful entrepreneur, a Certified Speaking Professional from the National Speakers Association, and author of *Personal Productivity Secrets* and *Work Without Walls*. She is a media favorite, featured weekly in a variety of national business outlets, including the *Wall Street Journal*, NPR, *Fast Company*, *Entrepreneur*, *Forbes*, *US News and World Report*, and the *Huffington Post*. She is also a regular contributor to the *Harvard Business Review*, with articles there viewed over a million times.

Maura earned an MBA from the University of Massachusetts and has studied the field of productivity all over the world for more than two decades.

Maura believes that every person has unique gifts to offer the world, and her purpose is to support them in offering those gifts in a way that is joyful and inspiring. She strives to have an impact that is relevant and unique, presenting new ideas and ways of thinking that are applicable to changing times.

Maura believes that her work should have a social impact on the world, so she is very active in her local community of Austin, Texas, where she has held volunteer leadership positions in a variety of different community organizations and charities. This belief also leads Maura to offer quarterly pro-bono presentations to nonprofits, to donate a percentage of all her revenues to charity, and to have volunteered as a Climate Project speaker (personally trained on the subject by former vice president and Nobel laureate Al Gore and his team of leading climate scientists).

NEW! Only from Simple Truths®

spark impact in just one hour

IGNITE READS IS A NEW SERIES OF 1-HOUR READS WRITTEN BY WORLD-RENOWNED EXPERTS!

These captivating books will help you become the best version of yourself, allowing for new opportunities in your personal and professional life. Accelerate your career and expand your knowledge with these powerful books written on today's hottest ideas.

TRENDING BUSINESS AND PERSONAL GROWTH TOPICS

 Read in an hour or less

 Leading experts and authors

 Bold design and captivating content

EXCLUSIVELY AVAILABLE ON SIMPLETRUTHS.COM

Need a training framework?
Engage your team with discussion guides and PowerPoints for training events or meetings.

Want your own branded editions?
Express gratitude, appreciation, and instill positive perceptions to staff or clients by adding your organization's logo to your edition of the book.

Add a supplemental visual experience
to any meeting, training, or event.

Contact us for special corporate discounts!
(800) 900-3427 x247 or simpletruths@sourcebooks.com

LOVED WHAT YOU READ AND WANT MORE?

Sign up today and be the FIRST to receive advance copies of Simple Truths® NEW releases written and signed by expert authors. Enjoy a complete package of supplemental materials that can help you host or lead a successful event. This high-value program will uplift you to be the best version of yourself!

— SIMPLE TRUTHS —
ELITE CLUB

ONE MONTH. ONE BOOK. ONE HOUR.

Your monthly dose of motivation, inspiration, and personal growth.